Celtic Prayers
FOR TIMES OF CRISIS

Celtic Prayers
FOR TIMES OF CRISIS

COMPILED BY ELLYN SANNA

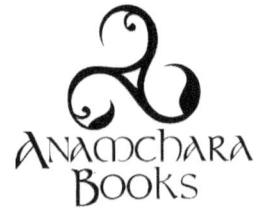

Copyright © Anamchara Books, 2020.

ANAMCHARA BOOKS
Vestal, New York 13850
www.AnamcharaBooks.com

IngramSpark 2020 paperback ISBN: 978-1-62524-806-0

Modern prayers unless otherwise noted are by Ellyn Sanna.

Cover illustration: *Splendor Solis*
by Salomon Trismosin, sixteenth century.

Celtic cross illustration: Migfoto (Dreamstime.com)

CONTENTS

Introduction   7

I. Prayers of Hope & Healing   11

II. Prayers of Blessing   29

III. Prayers for Courage & Strength   43

IV. Prayers for Protection   59

V. Prayers of Praise   85

Introduction

The word crisis has come to mean a time of intense difficulty, trouble, or danger—but the roots of the word point us in a slightly different direction. The Greek word *krisis* meant (according to *The Online Etymology Dictionary*) a "vitally important or decisive state of affairs; the point at which change must come, for better or worse." Related to disease, it meant the turning point: a change that indicated either recovery or death.

As we face the current crises in our world, we can keep that older definition in mind. These crises are not merely bad things we wish would go away. They can also be opportunities for change, for renewed health. Our response to crisis can make all the difference. Will we let it defeat us—or will we rise to the challenge and one day emerge from these catastrophic events as better people building a better world? Change must come; it is inevitable. But the form that change takes is at least partly up to us.

The prayers collected here offer us ways to spiritually meet the crises of our day. These prayers are written in the Celtic tradition. Many of them are modern, original poems written by Anamchara

Books' authors and staff; many are adapted from ancient Celtic prayers; and others are taken directly from original sources. The three sources we have used most are the *Carmina Gadelica*, a compendium of folk prayers, blessings, hymns, and lore collected by Alexander Carmichael from ordinary people living in Scotland between 1860 and 1909; *Ancient Irish Poetry,* translated by Kuno Meyer and published in 1911; and *The Poem Book of the Gael,* edited by Eleanor Hull and published in 1912. We have noted the source of each prayer that we've included.

Celtic spirituality is rooted in the past, but it is a real and growing presence in the twenty-first century. Regardless of the historicity of its roots (something debated by academic scholars), this form of spirituality has always belonged to ordinary people, rather than to any form of organized church or institution. It is a form of spirituality that is inclusive of all life, and Celtic prayers sweep together all that we are and all that we do, opening up to the Divine the entire experience of living. In the face of crisis, these prayers integrate body, mind, and soul into a single, holistic experience, an experience that is filled with the potential for spiritual growth and Divine action.

On her Facebook page, author Elizabeth Gilbert quotes a "Celtic Prayer of Approach":

> I honor your Gods,
> I drink at your well,
> I bring an undefended heart to our meeting place,
> I have no cherished outcomes,
> I will not negotiate by withholding, and
> I am not subject to disappointment.

As we stand in the midst of crisis, these affirmations are steep challenges. They call us to unite with others, without judgment, looking past the differences we have allowed to separate us. They ask us to share from each other's spiritual resources, and to let go of our own expectations, stepping outside of the rigid boxes that have defined us. In doing so, we give others room to find their full potential alongside us—and we also create Spirit space, a dynamic and living place where the Divine One meets us and works through us.

May each of the prayers in this book help us to meet these challenges.

—Ellyn Sanna

I
Prayers of Hope and Healing

"Hope," writes Rebecca Solnit, "is a gift you don't have to surrender, a power you don't have to throw away." It is not the same as optimism, and it is not a sunny, pie-in-the-sky attitude that insists everything is going to work out just fine. Hope sees the realities. It understands the very real dangers. But it also looks beyond the darkness and danger, and it sees possibilities. In Desmond Tutu's words, "Hope is being able to see that there is light despite all the darkness." Hope opens our hearts to Divine potential.

And hope goes hand in hand with healing. Healing brings wholeness to what is broken. It doesn't reverse the crisis; it doesn't undo the catastrophe. Instead, it rises out of crisis, giving meaning to even the worst circumstances. In the midst of danger and hardship, healing is what eventually emerges, bringing to life new strengths, creating something larger and better than we could ever have dreamed.

NEW BEGINNINGS

A modern prayer.

God of new beginnings,
may all that is coming to an end
give birth to something new.
Give us eyes to see a pregnant world;
give us ears to hear the groaning of Creation;
may we be midwifes to your new birth,
here, now, in this time of loss.
Enfold us all, your children here on Earth,
in the deep blue sky,
your living mantle of hope.
God of new beginnings,
give us hope.

WHEN I AM WOUNDED

Adapted from the Carmina Gadelica.

Put your salve on my sight,
put your balm on my wounds,
wrap your linen robe around my skin,
O Healing Hand, O Child of salvation.

O God of the weak,
O God of the lowly,
O God of the righteous,
O shield of homesteads.

You are calling me
with the voice of glory,
with the mouth of mercy
of the Beloved Child,
O may I find rest everlasting
in the home of your Trinity,
in the Paradise of your Peace,
in the Sun-Garden of your love.

WHEN WE ARE ILL

Adapted from the Carmina Gadelica.

Fairest One, you are the best medicine,
and your food is sweeter than all else.
Sustain and guide our bodies at every spot.
The knee that is stiff, O Healer, make pliant.
The heart that is hard make warm beneath your wing.
The soul that is wandering from your path,
grasp its helm and guide it back to life.
Each thing that is amiss in us, put right.
Each thing that is hard soften with your grace.
Each wound that is giving us pain,
O Best of Healers, make whole.

WHEN HEARTS ARE BROKEN

A modern prayer.

Let us have faith in the One
who built our life and limb,
the Maker of our mind and soul,
whose bright power is unfailing,
unending, without dimming.

O Bright Trinity of great power,
our hearts are broken.
Make us whole once more.

Our hearts are full of darkness.
Shine your light amid the shadows.
We are afraid to trust, lest we be hurt again.
Open our hearts, we pray,
so we may know your love.

Give us faith in you
Who built our life and limb,
The Maker of mind and soul,
whose bright power is unfailing,
unending, without dimming.

SOUL HEALING

A modern prayer.

All alone in my bed, with only the company of my soul,
I am on a pilgrimage through illness.
This sickness of my flesh is a journey I take.
It is my hermitage as well, a hidden place.
Here I draw away from the world, from my life,
from all that has occupied my mind and body.
Here I am alone with God.
Let this illness be a prayer.

Here ends all my talking, all my show, all my effort.
Here there is only sadness, loneliness, weakness.
This is the journey I take, a pilgrimage out of my life
through cold and barren lands.
I ask you, Holy One: meet me in this cell and heal me.
But before you heal my body, may this illness be a road
that leads me closer to you, Healer of my soul.

A PRAYER OF BRIGID

This modern prayer refers to God as the "Holy Housewife," which Jesus described in his parable of the lost coin, and likens the Divine to Brigid, goddess of home and hearth.

Grant me healing, O Life-Giver,
healing of nerve and bone, muscle and mind.
May your strong Spirit breathe in my every cell,
bringing renewal and energy to all that is sick and weak within me.

May all that is amiss within me be put right,
swept clean and scrubbed, by you, Holy Housewife,
with the help of sweet Brigid of the Fire.

I ask that Brigid tend my body's hearth,
the glowing fire at the center of my flesh.
With her help, may my heart-fire leap with new light,
to praise you, Giver of Life.

May Brigid, Lady of the Spring, bring renewal to my body.
May I burst forth with new life, like flowers after winter.
Grant me healing, O Life-Giver.
Bring renewal and energy to all that is sick and weak within me.

HEALING FOR THOUGHTS

Our thoughts have the power to magnify the seriousness of any situation, to rob us of peace, and to sap our strength, body, mind, and spirit. This prayer is based on a medieval Irish prayer.

Lord of Love, who loves me without limit,
I ask that you bring healing to my thoughts.
They stray constantly from your light,
following paths that lead only to anxiety and despair.

My willpower alone cannot constrain them;
as slippery as an eel's tail, they elude my grasp.
No lock nor fetter restrains them from their frantic course,
they lead me again and yet again into darkness.

O beloved Christ, to whom every thought is clear,
may the grace of the sevenfold Spirit keep my thoughts,
hold them in check when I cannot.
Rule my mind, O swift God of the elements,
that I may see the light of your love,
shining in my dark mind.

May my thoughts keep company with Christ and his companions;
may we be together—Brigid, Michael, Patrick, and Columba—
our thoughts united, in harmony with the Spirit of Truth,
who has grace and power to bring healing everywhere,
even to my thoughts.

HEALING FROM ALL THAT HOLDS ME BACK

Adapted from the Carmina Gadelica.

Three wishes I ask of the Good God when I arise today:
may I be healed of anxiety;
may my heart be at peace within me;
may I go forth in the courage of your Spirit.

Three prayers I ask of the Ruler of the Suns:
may I be healed of anger and resentment;
may I love all I see today;
may I carry forth your love to each and every soul I meet.

Three hopes I bring to the Ruler of the Stars:
may I be healed of shame;
may I know that I am loved by the Ruler of the Stars;
may I know that I am like snow, pure and without blemish.

Three graces I ask of the Bright Ruler of All:
may I be healed of all that holds me back;
may I walk in strength and love;
may I do your work upon this earth.

PRAYER FOR A WOUNDED EARTH

A modern prayer.

God who is Three-in-One,
we know you see the sparrow fall.
Surely, you see each polar bear that dies
as Earth's polar ice melts.
Christ who is the Lamb slain,
surely you feel the pain of dolphins,
rhinos, gorillas, whales, and turtles,
dying from the wounds
we have dealt your world.
God who is Mercy,
forgive us for our sins
against your world.

Give us eyes to see
that as we wounded the Earth,
we have wounded you
with our greed and ignorance.
Give us strength to change.
Bless each beast, bird, and fish,
each plant and tree,
each insect and microbe,
and each human
within your web of life.
Heal our wounds,
we pray.

HEALING DURING CLIMATE CHANGE

A modern prayer.

We pray, O Three-in-One,
for a world of rising temperatures,
drought and flood,
wild weather and broken seasons,
failed crops and dying forests.
Creator God, in your mercy,
renew this damaged world.

For each creature threatened by climate change,
we pray, O Three-in-One.
Creator God, in your mercy,
renew this damaged world.
You who made the Earth,
remake her now.
Give us love and strength
to partner with you
and renew this damaged world.

DIVINE MESSAGES

A modern prayer.

As the rain hides the stars,
as the autumn mist hides the hills,
as the clouds veil the blue of the sky,
so the dark happenings of my life
hide the shining of your face from me.
Yet the stars still shine behind the rain,
the hills are solid beneath the mist,
and when the wind drives the clouds away,
I see again the blue of Heaven.

As your Earth reminds me
again and yet again in all her changes
and in the wheel of her seasons,
you live beyond the momentary appearance
of my dark life.
Earth carries your message to me,
and it is enough,
for though I may stumble in my going,
you will not fall.

PRAYER TO THE EARTH

A modern prayer.

Earth, teach me humility
as blossoms are humble with beginning.
Earth, teach me courage
as the tree that stands alone.
Earth, teach me limitation
as the ant that crawls on the ground.
Earth, teach me freedom
as the eagle that soars in the sky.
Earth, teach me regeneration
as the seed that rises in the spring.
Earth, teach me to forget myself
as melted snow forgets its life.
Earth teach me hope,
as the bare trees wait for new leaves.

DIVINE REST

Adapted from a nineteenth-century Celtic folk prayer, this prayer speaks not only of our need for rest but also indicates that the Divine One rests with us, sharing our Sabbath times.

I rest with you, O Jesus,

as you rest yourself with me.

Christ's healing oil on my sad soul,

the breath of the Spirit to make me whole,

the Creator's love to set me free.

O Father-Mother, who created me,

O Word-Made-Flesh, who came down for me,

O Spirit Blest, who blesses me,

rest you with me.

PEACE

Adapted from the Carmina Gadelica.

And with the kindness
of the Heavenly Father, peace!
In the name of the Three
who are One, peace!
And by the will of the One
who rules wind and rain,
storm and sun,
the moon, the hills,
and all the Earth's round globe,
peace! Peace!

II
Prayers of Blessing

To bless means to confer goodness and abundance upon something. It is to acknowledge the sacredness of the thing which we bless, to affirm God's ability to work through it in ways that bring life (as when we "ask the blessing" on our food).

During times of crisis, we are called to do more than endure; we are called to actively bless the people and circumstances around us. In doing so, we open up events to the Divine hand. We not only allow God room to work, however, but we also become actively part of the process. In blessing others, we too are blessed, creating a chain strong enough to lead us through this crisis.

BLESSING IN A TIME OF ANXIETY

A modern prayer.

When your soul cries out in fear,
may the God of peace quiet you.

When the world shakes beneath your feet,
may the strength of stone hold you firm.

When lack and scarcity pinch your life,
may the rich green Earth nourish you.

When your body grows weak from exhaustion,
may the oak tree lend you strength.

When all seems lost,
may birdsong and sunlight give you hope.

When your soul quakes with anxiety,
may the Christ-Spirit enfold you,
and may Divine Love cast out all fear.

BLESS MY LIFE

Adapted from the Carmina Gadelica.

God, bless the world and all that is therein.
God, bless my family and my friends,
God, bless the eye that is in my head,
and bless, O God, all that my fingers touch.
What time I rise in the morning early,
what time I lie down late in bed,
bless my rising in the morning early,
and my lying down late in bed.

BLESSING

Adapted from the Carmina Gadelica.

When you feel the sun's light upon you,
may you be lit within your heart,
so that friends and strangers
will come and warm themselves,
as though a fire burned within you.
When you look up at the bright sky,
may its light enter you
and shine out from your two eyes,
like candles in the windows of a house,
showing the way to those who are lost.

When the cold rain falls on you,
may you feel its blessing,
so that it beats upon your spirit,
washing it fair and clean,
leaving within you a shining pool
that reflects the blue of Heaven,
and sometimes a star.
May the Earth bless you each day,
so that your heart is strengthened.
May you trust her as you trust God,
so that one day you will not be afraid
to give your body to her,
knowing she will keep you safe
until the day of your rising.

THE SHAPE OF CHRIST

Adapted from the Carmina Gadelica.

May God shield you on every steep,
may Christ aid you on every path,
may Spirit fill you on every slope.
May you find blessings on field and plain.
May the Ruler of Heaven shield you in the valleys,
may Christ aid you on the mountains,
may Spirit bathe you on the slopes.
in hollow, on hill, mountain, valley, and plain,
may you see writ the shape of Christ.

The shape of Christ be before you.
The shape of Christ be behind you.
The shape of Christ be over you.
The shape of Christ be under you.
The shape of Christ be with you.
The shape of Christ be around you.
In wind and cloud, light and rain,
in fog and chill, in sun and heat,
may you see writ the shape of Christ.

A PRAYER FOR A FRIEND

Adapted from the Carmina Gadelica.

May the blessing of light be on you—
the warm light of the sun,
the silver light of the moon,
the light of stars and running water,
and the light of God within your heart.
May the blessed light shine on you
and warm your heart
till it glows like a great peat fire.
May you see God's light on the path ahead
when the road you walk is dark.
May you always hear,
even in your hour of sorrow,
the sweet song of a bird outside your window.
When trouble comes,
may the summer rain be gentle on you,
and your heart not turn to stone.
Take comfort in the simple blessings
of fertile earth and shining sky,
and know through every sigh
you do not walk alone.

THE EARTH'S DEEP PEACE

From the Carmina Gadelica.

Deep peace I breathe into you,
O weariness, here:
O ache, here!
Deep peace, a soft white dove to you;
deep peace, a quiet rain to you;
deep peace, an ebbing wave to you!
Deep peace, red wind of the east from you;
deep peace, grey wind of the west to you;
deep peace, dark wind of the north from you;
deep peace, blue wind of the south to you!

Deep peace, pure red of the flame to you;
deep peace, pure white of the moon to you;
deep peace, pure green of the grass to you;
deep peace, pure brown of the earth to you;
deep peace, pure grey of the dew to you;
deep peace, pure blue of the sky to you!

Deep peace of the running wave to you;
deep peace of the flowing air to you;
deep peace of the quiet earth to you;
deep peace of the sleeping stones to you!

Deep peace of the shining stars to you;
deep peace of infinite space to you;
deep peace from the Son of Peace to you!
Deep peace from the heart of Mary to you,
and from Brigid of the Mantle,
deep peace, deep peace!

FOR A FRIEND WHO IS DISCOURAGED

A modern prayer.

My friend—may he know you made him without flaw.
Bright Lord of heaven and earth, bless his heart and mind.
Bring courage and light to all that is dark.

My friend—may she know you love her without measure.
Sweet Lord of Love, bless each moment of her day,
and bring her comfort and an upright spirit.

My friend—may he know that I am with him,
even though we are separated.
Make me your angel, a messenger,
bringing your hope and healing.

My friend—may she take strength
from morning light and evening's rest.
Enclose her in your Spirit's wings.

SAINT BRENDAN'S PRAYER

This prayer is attributed to Brendan the Voyager, who in the fifth century may have sailed as far as Iceland or even Newfoundland.

God, bless to me this day,
God bless to me this night;
bless, O bless, thou God of grace,
each day and hour of my life;
bless, O bless, thou God of grace,
each day and hour of my life.
God, bless the pathway on which I go;
God, bless the earth that is beneath my sole;
bless, O God, and give to me thy love,
O God of gods, bless my rest and my repose;
bless, O God, and give to me thy love,
and bless, O God of gods, my repose.

CIRCLE PRAYER

A modern prayer by Bruce Epperly.

Circle of love,

encompass my loved ones.

May your love well up within them.

May your passion enlighten them.

Circle of healing,

encompass my loved ones.

May your healing touch rest upon them.

May your light illumine them.

Circle of protection,

encompass my loved ones.

Surround them with your eternal safety.

Protect them from all temptations and ills.

Give them courage and strength

to live always from your safe and powerful center.

III
Prayers of Courage and Strength

To "take courage," in the oldest meaning of the phrase, meant "to take heart." The heart was considered to be the seat of personhood, what today we might call "the self," and so courage was intricately linked to selfhood. In other words, courage emerges when we are whole, our sense of self sure and firm. Without that inner certainty, we are easily shaken. In the midst of crisis, we may fall into pieces easily. We lack the interior core of strength to rise to the challenges of our day.

Selfhood is not, however, something that we ever achieve once and forever. Some of us may be farther along than others are on the continuum of inner strength, but all of us are still growing. If the current crisis makes us aware that we lack courage, that our inner core is easily thrown off balance, that self-knowledge can be the first step toward growth. As the apostle Paul wrote in his letter to the Romans, "In the midst of stress and pressure, I hold my head up high, knowing that this distress can bring about a patient enduring, an endurance that will prove my inner truth, and this inner truth will in turn bring about hope" (5:3,4). As we pray for strength and courage, we give the Divine One opportunity to work within us, lifting us up to new heights.

BREATH OF LIFE

A modern prayer

Breath of Life,
you are all around us and within us.
Breath of Life,
the rhythm of your life never ends.
Though life may seem to recede,
always it flows back again.
In the midst of crisis, we gasp for you;
you bend to us and breathe into us,
and we are renewed.
Breath of Life,
breathe in us,
so that in the midst of this crisis,
we may be renewed.

MY EVERY BREATH

Adapted from an ancient Gaelic prayer.

Thanks to you, O God,
that I have risen today,
to the rising of life itself.
Even now, in the midst of trouble and crisis;
may my life, my words, my every act,
my very breath be to your glory,
O God of every gift,
and to the glory of my soul likewise.

Glory, O great One, is the living light
that shines from your heart into mine.
Thank you that your light never dims,
even when my vision grows cloudy with fear.

O great God, aid my soul
with the aiding of your own light.
Even as I clothe my body with wool,
cover my soul with the shadow of your wing.
Guard my heart from fear,
and as the mist scatters on the crest of the hills,
may each ill haze clear from my soul, O God.
May my every breath be to your glory.

HOLY MYSTERY

A modern prayer.

O Holy Mystery, all-loving God,
open my heart to hear your Voice
through the cries of a wounded world,
to see your Face
in the midst of a darkened world.

O Holy Mystery, all-healing God,
use me to repair a broken world,
to speak truth in the midst of confusion,
to work hand-in-hand with Blessed Brigid,
bringing comfort to a world of sorrow.

O Holy Mystery, do your will, work your way,
unseen, unheard,
in the midst of our wounded world,
in the midst of our darkened world,
in the midst of our broken world.

THE ACORN

A modern prayer.

O Love Beyond All Loves,
you see that the acorn lies like a stone,
quiet, hard, self-contained, and lifeless.
My heart feels like a stone,
quiet, hard, self-contained, nearly lifeless.
Yet deep in the soil, beneath the storms of life,
the acorn softens, cracks, opens,
and shoots out life.

May my own heart now, in the storms of life,
grow soft beneath the rain,
crack open from life's blows,
and begin to grow.
The strong-hearted oak
grows from the tiny acorn.
May my own life grow out from my broken heart,
tall and bright, full of courage and love,
a spreading tree to give you glory,
O Love Beyond All Loves

BRIGHT MORNING STAR

A modern prayer.

Kindle your flame in us,
Living One.
May we burn ever brighter,
even now, even in the dark.
Bright Morning Star,
light of our eyes, joy of our night,
shine in our hearts,
even now, even in the dark.

WANDERING THOUGHTS

This tenth-century Irish prayer shows us that wandering thoughts are nothing new. The Celtic saints knew all about what meditation experts call the "monkey mind."

Shame to my thoughts, how they stray from me!
They fill me with the fear of danger,
as though I faced the day of eternal doom.
When I try to pray, they wander on a trackless path;
they fret, they whine, they misbehave.
Through eager crowds, through pleasures and griefs,
through woods, through cities—swifter they are than the wind.
Now through paths of loveliness, and then through darkness deep!
Without a ferry or ever missing a step,
they go across every sea;
swiftly they leap in one bound from earth to heaven.

They run a race of folly anear and afar;
though I try to bind them or put shackles on their feet,
they pay me no mind.
Great Giver of Life who rules the stars,
what can I do but give to you
my wandering thoughts?
Only you can keep pace with them,
only you can bring me peace.
O Beloved, O Truth, to whom every eye is clear,
may the grace of the seven-fold Spirit come to my thoughts
to keep them, to check them!
Rule this heart of mine, O God of the elements,
that you will be my love, and I the same to you.
That I may reach Christ and all Heaven's companions,
who are neither fickle nor inconstant
but more steady than the stars.

COME, SPIRIT!

A modern prayer by Zachary Chastain.

As I look into the glass,
I see no light inside this face,
and yet you breathed life into this fragile thing,
my self;
into this little portion,
you breathed your Spirit, O Creator God.
But how quickly, how easily I tire.
Rescue me from vanity—
and self-loathing too.

Kindle light within me,
and increase your glory:
come, Spirit!
Free my blood to beat calmly in my breast:
come, Spirit!
Humble me and make me unafraid to face the world:
come, Spirit!
bring me into union with you,
O Unity in Trinity, O Trinity in Unity.
I call out to you:
come, Spirit!

HUNGRY

A modern prayer by Sheila Stewart.

I am empty, O God.
My body craves the food it needs.
My soul craves the food it needs.
My mind craves the food it needs.

A growling stomach,
despair and loneliness,
boredom and unrest.
These are the signs of my hunger.

Fill me, O my God.
Strengthen my body with bread and fruit.
Strengthen my soul with love and friendship.
Strengthen my mind with truth and conversation.

Let me not forget that others hunger too.
Let me not forget that body, soul, and mind
must all be fed.
Let me not deny my hunger.

Give me the means to feed others, O God.
As Christ multiplied the bread and fish,
multiply nourishment through me.
And let me nourish those around me.

MERCY AND JUSTICE

Adapted from the Carmina Gadelica.

May I speak each day according to your justice,
each day may I show your authority, O God;
may I speak each day according to your wisdom,
each day and night may I be at peace with you.

Each day may I count the causes of your mercy,
may I each day give heed to your laws;
each day may I compose for you a song,
may I harp each day your praise, O God.
may I each day give love to you, Jesu.

Each night may I do the same;
each day and night, dark and light,
may I praise your goodness to me, O God.

TODAY'S WORK

Adapted from the Carmina Gadelica.

Today, I will do my day's work
as would Mary, mother of Jesus,
never forgetting to look up and see the sky.
I will travel to my next place
in the presence of the angels,
seeing their wings among the trees.
Who is near me when I am sad and alone?
It is Jesus, the King of the sun,
who breathes his love on the wind
and sings comfort
in every sparrow's song.

EBB AND FLOW

Adapted from the Carmina Gadelica.

With the ebb, with the flow
of sea and tide,
teach me thy patience.
Teach me that as it was,
as it is, as it shall be
evermore,
are all an ebb and flow
of thy grace.
With the ebb, with the flow,
of earth and sea,
remind me, O Thou Triune,
that Thy grace has no need of hurry.
With the ebb, with the flow,
so shall it be
evermore.

SONG OF THE SEA

Even today, long centuries after this ancient Irish prayer was written, weather can still be a fearsome thing, smashing our sense of security. Symbolically as well, storms of all sorts shake our world—and yet this prayer challenges us to find the exhilaration of cleaving the waves with God.

A great tempest rages across the Earth,
bold to cross all borders.
Wind has arisen, fierce winter has slain us;
it has come across the sea, it has pierced us like a spear.
The ocean is in flood, the sea is full,
and yet—delightful is the home of ships,
and as the wind whirls the sand across the beach,
swiftly the ship rudder cleaves the broad sea.

O Beloved One, save me from the horror of fierce tempests.
Great Lord of the Feast, teach me to ride the waves
aboard your craft.
Now I shall I launch my little coracle
on the broad-bosomed glorious ocean.
I shall go, O Ruler of bright Heaven,
of my own will upon the brine.
O God, stand by me
as I venture out into the sea.

IV
Prayers for Protection

The Latin root words for *protect* meant "to cover in front." Imagine yourself holding one of the large round shields that Celtic warriors carried. Behind this shield, you are safe from the onslaught of the enemy's blows. Although it cannot cover every piece of your body, it covers your heart, the centermost part of you, the inner core of who you are.

These prayers for protection affirm the Divine power to cover us, shielding us from harm. We are not immune to the dangers around us; we will not magically be lifted above them. And yet our innermost being is safe, shielded by the One who loves us.

A PLEA

Adapted from Ancient Irish Poetry.

Living One, I ask that you
lean down and listen to my plea.
Let my prayers ascend upward,
as you protect me downward.
Come, O Bright Glory,
from north, from south,
from east, from west,
and surround me with protection.
O Ruler of Life, O Giver of Mercy,
O Bright Star, O Love Unending,
protect me with power.

THE SOUL PLAINT

Adapted from Ancient Irish Poetry.

O Beloved! tonight,
O Shepherd of the poor,
save me from evil,
save me from harm.
O save my body,
sanctify me tonight,
O Beloved! tonight,
do not leave me.
Endow me with strength,
O Herdsman of might.
Guide me aright,
guide me in your strength,
O Beloved! in your strength
preserve me.

GOD'S SANCTUARY

Adapted from the Carmina Gadelica.

I am placing my soul and my body
on your sanctuary, O God,
on your sanctuary, O Beloved,
on your sanctuary, O Spirit of perfect truth,
the Three who would defend my cause,
and not turn their backs upon me.

O Creator, who is kind and just,
O Child, who overcame death,
O Spirit of power,
keep me from harm;
the Three who would justify me,
keep me this day and night and always.

THE SOUL SHRINE

Adapted from the Carmina Gadelica. The "soul shrine" was a term used for the home—a sacred resting place for the soul.

Beloved, give charge to your blessed angels,
to keep guard around this home tonight,
a band sacred, strong, and steadfast,
that will shield this soul shrine from harm.

Safeguard, O Beloved, this household tonight,
its people, their resources, and their reputations,
and deliver them from death, from distress, from harm,
from the fruits of envy and of hatred.

Give to us, O God of peace,
thankfulness despite our loss,
to obey your will here below,
And to enjoy you above.

ENCIRCLING PRAYER

Adapted from the Carmina Gadelica.

My Christ, my shield, my encircler,
each day, each night, each light, each dark.
My Christ, my Christ! My shield, my encircler,
each day, each night, each light, each dark,
be near me, uphold me, my Treasure, my Triumph,
in my lying, in my standing, in my watching, in my sleeping,
Jesus, Son of David, my strength everlasting!
Jesus, Son of Mary, my helper, my encircler!

THE GUARDIAN ANGEL

Adapted from the Carmina Gadelica.

O angel of God who has charge of me
from the dear Creator of mercy,
make 'round about me this night
the shepherd's fold of the saints.
Drive from me every temptation and danger,
surround me on the sea of unrighteousness,
and in the narrows, crooks, and straits,
keep my small boat, keep it always.
Be a bright flame before me,
be a guiding star above me,
be a smooth path below me,
And be a kindly shepherd behind me,
today, tonight, and forever.
I am tired and I am a stranger;
lead me to the land of angels.
It is time for me to go home
to the court of Christ, to the peace of Heaven.

CHRIST'S CROSS

Adapted from the Carmina Gadelica. The cross is an important symbol for Celtic spirituality, representing not only the instrument of Jesus' death but also the intersection of heaven and earth, a holy place of possibility and hope. This prayer makes the sign of the cross over all reality.

Christ's cross over this face I wear, and over my ear.

Christ's cross over my eye.

Christ's cross over my nose.

Christ's cross to accompany me before.

Christ's cross to accompany me behind me.

Christ's cross to meet every difficulty
both on hollow and hill.

Christ's cross eastwards facing me.

Christ's cross back toward the sunset.

In the north, in the south,

increasingly may Christ's cross straightway be.

Christ's cross up to broad Heaven.

Christ's cross down to Earth.

Let no evil or hurt come to my body or my soul.
Christ's cross over me as I sit.
Christ's cross over me as I lie.
Christ's cross be all my strength
until we reach the King of Heaven.
From the top of my head to the end of my toenail,
O Christ, against every danger
I trust in the protection of the cross.
Till the day of my death,
when my flesh goes into the clay,
and I shall once more take
Christ's cross over this face.

WHEN I AM BESIEGED

A modern prayer.

Help me, Unity in Trinity,
Trinity in Unity, I beseech you,
for I am in peril.
My mind is besieged by the television,
my heart is trapped by busyness,
and my body grows weak from lack of use.
I ask the high powers of the hosts of heaven
not to leave me here lost in my life.
Defend me, I pray,
from stress and depression,
Christ, my heart's true love.
Guard me, I ask,
from gossip and unkind words,
Bright God of the High Heavens.
Breathe through me, I beg you, Spirit of God,
that my body may be whole and strong,
and my heart full of your joy.
Help me, Unity in Trinity,
Trinity in Unity, I beseech you.

THE SHIELD OF GOD

Adapted from the Carmina Gadelica.

God of Heaven, God of Earth,
hold your shield over us, protect us all,
Jesu beloved!
Creator of the Shining Ones!
Shield, oh shield us
in the arms of the Earth.
Safeguard our animals,
the small ones we love,
encircle us together.
You walk the trackways of power
across the Earth,
you guide the stars.

Guide well ourselves,
and shield, we pray,
the great and ancient procession
of life across your Earth.
O Creator! O Father!
O Mother! O Christ!
O Spirit! O Wisdom!
Be the Triad with us day and night,
on fertile field and rocky mountain ridge.
Be the Triad who is One
and wrap Earth's cloak of air around us.
May we feel your shield
in snowfall and winter gloom,
in green buds and springtime joy,
in the heat of summer days
and in autumn's sweet abundance.
Be with us in each one
and wrap your love around us.
O Three in One,
wrap your love around us.

A PRAYER OF PROTECTION FOR THE EARTH

A modern prayer by Kenneth McIntosh.

O Threefold Maker of Wonders,
as thou art the Spirit within all things green
guard thou the air-giving forests,
curb those who belch toxic emissions.
Thou Shield of Protection, guard us forever.
Be thou a force of strong conscience
to shield us securely from destroying the Earth,
from the corporations and the need to exploit,
and from our own greedy natures.
O thou who sustains the very air we breathe,
as thou art the Spirit in all things green,
save us from our folly.
Call us to thy aid.

PRAYER OF PROTECTION

From The Poem Book of the Gael.

In each space between,
in the darkness of night,
keep me safe with you, O Living One,
in the eternal kingdom,
where there is flaming radiance forever.
On each day of sun and cloud,
may the Trinity protect me!
In each night of dark,
may the Trinity defend me!
May the Trinity save me from every hurt,
from every danger!

THE PROTECTION OF GOD

This nineteenth-century Celtic folk prayer adapted from The Poem Book of the Gael *speaks of the safety and rest that can be found while identifying with the world's marginalized.*

I myself lie down with God,
may God lie down with me!
The protection of God above my head,
and the cross of the angels beneath my body.

Where will you lie down tonight?
With the poor and rejected,
who lie in pain and need.
Why will you lie down there and sleep?
Because lying there, I rest between Mary and her Son,
between bright Brigid and her mantle,
between Michael and his shield.

Where will you arise on the morrow?
I will arise with Patrick.
Who will you see in front of you?
Two hundred angels.
Who will be behind you?
As many again of the people of God.

O you who are shedding tears,
look and see—
Mary and her Son are between you and your fears.
Brigid with her mantle,
Michael with his shield,
and the two long hands of God enfolding us all,
that is what lies between you and each grief,
always and always, all through the years.

So lie you down with God,
and may God lie down with you!
The protection of God above your head,
and the cross of the angels beneath your body,
always and always, all through the years.

DIVINE NAVIGATOR

From the Carmina Gadelica.

God the Father, all-powerful, all loving,
Jesus, the Son of tears and sorrow,
with thy co-assistance, O Holy Spirit!
The Three-One, ever-living, ever-mighty, everlasting,
who brought the Children of Israel through the Red Sea,
and Jonah to land from the belly
of the great creature of the ocean,
who brought Paul and his companions in the ship,
from the torment of the sea, from the sorrow of the waves,
from the great gale, from the heavy storm,
protect us and shield and sanctify us.
Be seated, O Ruler of the elements, at our helm,
and lead us in peace to the end of our journey.

CAIM

Circling prayers, also known as Caim prayers (from the Gaelic meaning "protection" or "sanctuary") are used to create a ring of safety around yourself. It is an ancient Celtic form of prayer that often involves drawing a literal circle. The circle can be extended, however, to include your home, your community, even the entire planet.

Circle me, Beloved.

Keep protection near and danger afar.

Circle me, Beloved.

Keep light near and darkness afar.

Circle me, Beloved.

Keep peace within, keep evil out.

Circle me, Beloved.

Keep hope within, keep fear without.

Circle me, Beloved.

Keep love within, keep hate without.

Circle me, Beloved.

Keep truth within, keep lies without.

Circle me, Beloved.

Keep friendship within,

keep intolerance without.

Circle me, Beloved.

Keep health near and illness afar.

May you be a bright flame before me.
May you be a guiding star above me.
May you be a smooth path below me,
and a loving Guide behind me,
today, tonight, and forever.

SAINT PATRICK'S BREASTPLATE

This prayer of protection is attributed to Saint Patrick. It is also sometimes called "The Deer's Cry," because Patrick is said to have sang this when he was hiding from enemies—who passed by Patrick and his companion, seeing only a herd of deer. It is a powerful shield against the forces of evil.

I arise today
through a mighty strength,
the invocation of the Trinity,
through belief in the Threeness,
through confession of the Oneness
of the Creator of creation.

I arise today
through the strength of Christ's birth and baptism,
through the strength of Christ's crucifixion and burial,
through the strength of Christ's resurrection and ascension.

I arise today
through the strength of the love of cherubim,
through the obedience of angels,
through the service of archangels,
in the hope of resurrection,
in the prayers of matriarchs and patriarchs,

in the predictions of prophets,
in the preaching of apostles,
in the faith of confessors,
in the innocence of children,
in the courage of people of justice everywhere.

I arise today, through
the strength of heaven,
the light of the sun,
the radiance of the moon,
the splendor of fire,
the speed of lightning,
the swiftness of wind,
the depth of the sea,
the stability of the earth,
the firmness of rock.

I arise today, through
God's strength to pilot me,
God's might to uphold me,
God's wisdom to guide me,
God's eye to look before me,
God's ear to hear me,
God's word to speak for me,

God's hand to guard me,
God's shield to protect me,
God's host to save me
from snares and temptations,
from everyone who wishes me ill,
afar and near.

I summon today
all these powers between me and those evils,
against every cruel and merciless power
that may oppose my body and soul,
against everything that could wound me body and soul;
Christ to shield me today
against poison, against illness,
against accident, against wounding,
so that I may be entirely safeguarded.

Christ with me,
Christ before me,
Christ behind me,
Christ in me,
Christ beneath me,
Christ above me,
Christ on my right,
Christ on my left,
Christ when I lie down,
Christ when I sit down,
Christ when I arise,
Christ in the heart of everyone who thinks of me,
Christ in the mouth of everyone who speaks of me,
Christ in every eye that sees me,
Christ in every ear that hears me.

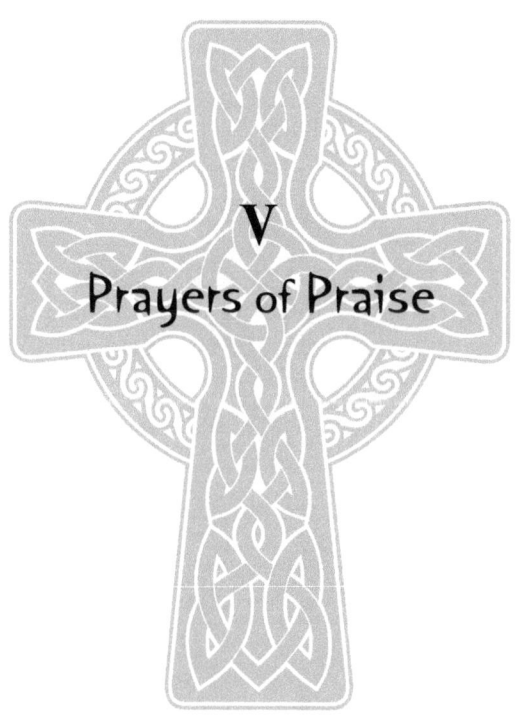

V
Prayers of Praise

Praise is not something an egotistical male God craves from his servants. Instead, praise is a natural function of the human soul. It is the recognition and celebration of life's deep-down goodness, even when the world is full of darkness.

Praising, even in the midst of a crisis, is good for our soul-health. It affirms that no matter how bad things look, the universe is held safe within Spirit's embrace. It opens our hearts to joy. It allows us to see past the ever-present reality of the crisis. Etty Hillesum (who died in the Holocaust) wrote, "As life becomes harder and more threatening, it also becomes richer, because the fewer expectations we have, the more the good things of life become unexpected gifts that we accept with gratitude."

May we see life's richness, even now, even here.

THE DIVINE HOST

A modern prayer.

Generous Host,
you call us to your table,
even now, in the presence of our enemies.

As the sun blesses all the Earth,
you bless us in joy and hardship.
As the wind circles the Earth,
you circle us with your peace.
As your creatures find nourishment
from your hand,
you nourish us without stinting.
As the waters encompass the Earth,
you encompass us with love.

Generous Host,
call us to the table,
even now, in the presence of our enemies.

GOD OF THREENESS

A modern prayer.

God of Threeness,
Creator, Christ, and Spirit,
you bless the spaces between us,
the bonds that connect us,
the relationships that link us.

God of Threeness,
in this time of darkness,
strengthen the bonds that connect us,
bless the relationships that link us,
and unite us in your love.

God of Threeness,
Creator, Christ, and Spirit,
united by love, linked by relationship,
a dance that never ends,
even now amid the darkness.

PRAISE FOR HEALING

A modern prayer.

Blessing and brightness,
wisdom and insight,
renewed power and well-being,
come from the One who lives within all.

Rest and heart's ease,
peace and sweet sleep,
freedom from tension,
all come from the Spirit, Living Breath.

Joy and contentment,
love without bounds,
friendship unfailing,
come from Jesus, my heart's Brother.

Blessing everlasting
to heal every woe,
mend every illness,
lift up weary hearts,
strengthen weak bodies,
and lighten every trouble,
these come from the Three-in-One,
Holy Trinity, source of bright blessing.

GOD IN THE EVERYWHERE

Adapted from the Carmina Gadelica.

You are the peace of all things calm.
You are the place to hide from harm.
You are the light that shines in dark.
You are the heart's eternal spark.
You are the door that's open wide.
You are the guest who waits inside.
You are the stranger at the door.
You are the calling of the poor.
You are my Beloved and with me still.
You are my love, keep me from ill.
You are the light, the truth, the way.
You are my Beloved this very day.

HOLY CREATOR OF GLORY

Adapted from the Carmina Gadelica.

Thanks be to you, Holy Creator of Glory,
Creator kind, ever-loving, ever-powerful,
because of all the abundance, favor, and deliverance
that you give us in our need.
Whatever circumstances happen to us as your children,
in our portion, in our lot, in our path,
give to us also the rich gifts of your hand
and the joyous blessing of your mouth.
Send forth to us the power of your love,
leap over the mountains of our transgressions,
and wash us in the true blood of conciliation,
like the moss of the mountain, like the lily on the lake.

In the steep common path of our calling,
be it easy or uneasy to our flesh,
be it bright or dark for us to follow,
your own perfect guidance be upon us.
Shield us from the wiles of the deceiver,
from the arch-destroyer with his arrows pursuing us,
and in each secret thought our minds do weave,
stand at our helm and at our sail.

Now to the Creator who made each creature,
now to the Son who united himself with all people,
now to the Holy Spirit, Comforter of might—
shield and protect us from every wound.
be in the beginning and end of our race;
let us sing in glory,
in peace, in rest, in reconciliation,
where no tear shall be shed, where death comes no more.
where no tear shall be shed, where death comes no more.

TALIESEN'S PRAYER OF BEAUTY

This Welsh poem is ascribed to the sixth-century bard Taliesen.

Beautiful it is that God shall save me.
Beautiful too the bright fish in the lake,
beautiful too the sun in the sky,
the beauty of an eagle on the shore when the tide is full,
the beauty of desire and the love between lovers,
beautiful too a gift which is loved,
beautiful too the moon shining on the Earth,
the beauty of summer, its days long and slow,
the beauty of flowers on fruit trees,
beautiful the covenant of the Creator with Earth,
the beauty in the wilderness of doe and fawn,
the beauty of wild leeks and the berries of harvest,
the beauty of the heather when it turns purple,
beautiful the pastureland,
beautiful too the beasts who suckle their young,
the beauty of water shimmering,
the beauty of the world where the Trinity speaks,
but the loveliest of all is the Christ
who lives in all beauty.

BLESSINGS EVERYWHERE

A modern prayer by Kenneth McIntosh.

The oak tree blesses me,
O God of strength.
The stone in my hand blesses me,
O God who endures.

The bird on the wing blesses me,
O God of freedom.
The deer in the forest blesses me,
O God of gentleness.

The abundance of bluebells on the hills
blesses me,
O God of bounty.
Starlight and moonlight bless me,
O God of quiet illumination.

The wind in the trees blesses me,
O God of Spirit-Breath.
The rain on my face blesses me,
O God who cleanses me.
Each thing I see blesses me,
O God who loves me.

BE THOU MY VISION

This prayer, which has become a well-known hymn, comes from a Middle Irish poem often attributed to the sixth-century poet Saint Dallán Forgaill. This English version, with some minor variations, was translated by Eleanor Hull and was included in The Poem Book of the Gael.

Be thou my Vision, O Lord of my heart,
naught is all else to me, save that thou art.
Thou my best thought by day and by night,
Waking or sleeping, thy presence my light.

Be thou my Wisdom, thou my true Word;
I ever with thee, thou with me, Lord.
Thou my great Parent, I thy dear child;
thou in me dwelling, a Threeness so wild.

Be thou my battle-shield, sword for the fight,
Be thou my dignity, thou my delight.
Thou my soul's shelter, thou my high tower;
raise thou me heavenward, Power of my power.

Riches I heed not or the world's empty praise,
thou mine inheritance now and always.
Thou, and thou only, first in my heart,
High Ruler of Heaven, my treasure thou art.

Ruler of the seven heavens, grant me for dole,
thy love in my heart, thy light in my soul.
Thy light from my soul, thy love from my heart,
Ruler of the seven heavens, may they never depart.

With the High Ruler of heaven, after victory won,
May I reach heaven's joys, O Bright Heaven's Sun!
Heart of my own heart, whatever befall,
still be my Vision, O Ruler of all.

Tree of Life

Celtic Prayers to the Universal Christ

Christ is the visible image of the invisible God.
He existed before anything was created and is supreme over all
creation, for through him God created everything. . . .
He existed before anything else, and he holds all creation together.
—Colossians 1:15–17

Like a vast, ever-growing Tree of Life, Christ—the expression of Divine love—expands endlessly throughout the universe. This is the perspective of ancient Celtic spirituality, and it is this concept that Ray Simpson reveals in his poem-prayers. Inspired by the traditional Celtic style of prayer, he gives words to our individual

relationships with God. He speaks of the wonder, beauty, and love revealed through the Universal Christ, the Tree of Life that includes all that is. Each and everything in creation is sacred, for everything is a word of God—and we too are called to be God's words to our world.

Paperback Price: $19.99

Kindle Price: $5.99

The Celtic Book of Days

Ancient Wisdom for Each Day of the Year from the Celtic Followers of Christ

This book will change the way you look at everyday life.

The ancient Celts found God's presence in each ordinary moment of the day. Everything they encountered revealed to them the presence of the sacred; each day was deep with meaning. Now you too can practice the Celts' faith, as you take a few moments to immerse yourself in their wisdom. These small daily moments of reflection and insight will open your heart to each day and all it holds.

Paperback Price: $28.99

Kindle Price: $9.99

Water from an Ancient Well

Celtic Spirituality for Modern Life

A Fresh Look at Celtic Spirituality

Using story, scripture, reflection, and prayer, this book offers readers a taste of the living water that refreshed the ancient Celts. The author invites readers to imitate the Celtic saints who were aware of God as a living presence in everybody and everything. This ancient perspective gives radical new alternatives to modern faith practices, ones that are both challenging and constructively positive. This is a Christianity big enough to embrace the entire world.

Paperback Price: $19.99

Kindle Price: $7.49

All Shall Be Well

A Modern-Language Version of the Revelation of Julian of Norwich

The fourteenth-century mystic, Julian of Norwich, was intimately acquainted with the Feminine Spirit. She wrote: "Mercy is an act of compassion that expresses God's Motherhood, the Divine Feminine who is tender and loving. . . . God rejoices that He is our Father, and at the same time She rejoices that She is our Mother." Julian goes on to say, "I understood that we can consider God's Motherhood from three perspectives: the first is that the Divine Mother gave birth to us and gave us life; the second is that She shared our lives; and the third is that She works always to keep us safe."

The great spiritual classic by Julian of Norwich is now available in modern, easy-to-comprehend language that stays true to Julian's original meanings. Discover Julian's joyous affirmation of the certainty of Divine love, a love that overcomes all.

Paperback Price: $24.95

Kindle Price: $9.99

AnamcharaBooks.com

www.ingramcontent.com/pod-product-compliance
Lightning Source LLC
Chambersburg PA
CBHW060535080526
44586CB00012B/746